Croft Castle

Herefordshire

THE NATIONAL TRUST

Picturesque antiquity

You approach Croft Castle across the tranquil, deeply rural landscape of north Herefordshire. An avenue of gnarled oak and beech trees leads through the Gothic arch of the curtain wall to the entrance front of the castle and the little church of St Michael. Battlements and corner towers speak of antiquity.

And Croft *is* genuinely ancient. There have been settled communities farming the area since the Iron Age. Almost thirty generations of the Croft family, who took their name from the place, have lived here over the last thousand years, and they live here still. But what we see today has been subtly enhanced to look more picturesquely ancient.

The present castle was built, not in the Middle Ages as you might imagine, but in the early 17th century, and is an important early example of the medieval revival. After the castle was dismantled during the Civil War, the Crofts rebuilt it in more or less the same form. In the 1760s, many of the principal rooms were

Key moments

Early 17th century	Present castle built
1660s	Castle repaired by Herbert Croft, Bishop of Hereford, after it had been dismantled during the Civil War
1746	Sir Archer Croft, 2nd Bt, sells Croft to Richard Knight, who passed it to his daughter Elizabeth and her husband, Thomas Johnes I
1760s	Shropshire architect T.F. Pritchard redecorates the interior in Gothick style
1923	Crofts repurchase Croft Castle
1957	Croft Castle handed over to the National Trust

redecorated in a Gothic revival style that also looks back to the Middle Ages for inspiration, but at the same time they were fitted with elegant, and convenient, Georgian sash-windows. Outside, a Gothic mood permeates the Picturesque irregularity of the Fish Pool Valley and the curtain wall, built around 1810.

The link between the Crofts and Croft Castle seemed to have come to an end in 1746, when they sold the estate, but such was the tug of ancient roots that 177 years later, in 1923, the Crofts decided to repurchase the estate. The next 30 years were difficult, but thanks to the determination of the 2nd Lord Croft and his family and the support of the National Trust and the National Land Fund, the estate was held together and opened for all to enjoy.

The entrance front of the castle stands close to St Michael's church

Gothick style

This was the first, 18th-century phase of the Gothic Revival. In 1753 William Whitehead remarked, 'A few years ago everything was Gothic: our houses, our beds, our bookcases, and our couches, were all copied from some parts or other of our old cathedrals.' The style's most recognisable form is the Gothic arch, and it is generally more spindly and less archaeologically correct than Victorian Gothic. It was often combined, as at Croft, with the curling ornament of the Rococo style.

Croft Castle has a fine collection of chairs in the Gothick style, most of which can be seen in the Gallery.

Tour of the Castle

The Exterior

The plan of Croft Castle is simple – roughly square, with a circular tower at each corner around an open central courtyard. But the architectural history of the building is much more complicated. The original early 17th-century fabric had to be reconstructed after the castle was reduced to a shell during the Civil War. It was re-Gothicised in the 1760s, altered again in 1913, and reduced in size in 1937. The result is an intriguing patchwork of periods and styles.

The East (Entrance) Front

There may originally have been a forecourt with an inner gatehouse in the centre of this front, through which horses would have passed to reach the central courtyard. If so, it disappeared during the Civil War. The present range, with its sash-windows and two pretty Gothick bays, was designed by T. F. Pritchard in the 1760s. Finally, in 1913 Walter Sarel added the entrance porch, obscuring Pritchard's more elegant front door.

The South Front

This side of the castle enjoys the best views and overlooks the battlemented terrace, which was built about 1810 on the site of the 17th-century formal garden. This roofline was simplified in 1913, when Sarel removed the battlements.

The West Front

On this side of the house, the roof is hidden by a parapet and false windows, which contain panes of mauve glass similar to that found at Hafod (see p. 34). At the north-west corner you can still see the stump of the 17th-century brick service wing demolished in 1937 to reduce the castle to a more manageable size.

The North Front

This range runs at a slightly oblique angle to the others, and is the least altered of the four. The right-hand block contains a 17th-century staircase, and the unsymmetrical arrangement of mullioned windows gives the best idea of what the castle would originally have looked like.

The castle from the south-west in 1834, when it still had its castellated gables. To the left is the service wing, which was demolished in 1937

The castle from the south-west today

(Left) The entrance front as it was before 1913, when the porch was added and the battlements were removed from the roof

The Interior

The Hall

This may look like one of the oldest rooms in the castle, but it is in fact among the most recent.

When this room was created in the mid-18th century as part of the new east range, it was probably given the same decorative treatment as the Gothick Staircase. In 1913 the tenants of the Kevill-Davies family (the then owners) commissioned the architect Walter Sarel to sweep all this away, replacing it with a blander, 'Old English' scheme, which they must have thought was more appropriate to an ancient castle. As a result, however, the Hall now seems slightly out of keeping with the other main rooms, which retain their 18th-century Gothick decoration.

The *17th-century panelling* was introduced in 1913, supplemented by new to match. The massive *stone inglenook fireplace* and the glazed screen opposite were installed at the same time.

Above the screen doors is the Croft coat of arms in stained glass.

Pictures

Several of the *portraits* here recall the Elizabethan era of *Sir James Croft* (d. 1590), who is shown holding his staff of office as Controller of Elizabeth I's Household in the portrait to the left of the fireplace. Croft had refused to implicate the young Elizabeth in Wyatt's Rebellion against Queen Mary in 1554. So after

Charles I as Prince of Wales

of the Crofts, who lived through the Civil War. *Herbert Croft, Bishop of Hereford* (1603–91) (left of the fireplace) began his career as Catholic chaplain to *Charles I* (portrayed as Prince of Wales right of the fireplace). As Dean of Hereford, he bravely continued to preach against the desecration of the cathedral, even when Parliamentary soldiers levelled their muskets at him. He largely rebuilt the castle following the Civil War. There are also images of his elder brother, *Colonel Sir James Croft* (d. 1659), and their sister *Elizabeth*, who married Sir Thomas Cave of Stamford. Their eldest brother, *Sir William* (1593–1645), who was killed during the Civil War, is represented here by his *pike*.

Sir James Croft, 11th Bt (in the inglenook on the right) was painted by J. P. Barraclough in 1925, two years after his trustees had bought back the Croft estate sold by his ancestors more than 150 years before. He was killed in 1941 while on active service with the Commandos. The portrait above depicts his sister Belinda standing in the upstairs corridor at Croft.

Furniture

The oak furniture is mainly 17th-century, including a two-storey *court cupboard*, which was used for displaying silver or for serving food.

The four *intricately carved tableaux* in heavy frames in the left-hand window recess were the work of Cornelis Bavelaar (1785–1835) of Leiden.

she became Queen, she gratefully defended Croft when he fell out with many of her senior courtiers. Her chief minister, **Lord Burghley** (next to the entrance door), commented that the prickly Croft was his own worst enemy: 'the man has not the readiest way to do good to himself'. Croft also argued with one of the Queen's most powerful intimates, *Robert Dudley, Earl of Leicester* (left of Sir James Croft); indeed, Croft's son Edward was accused of employing a conjuror to cast spells to bring about Leicester's death in 1588.

Other portraits depict the mid-17th-century generation

(Left) The Hall

(Right) A family upset; one of Cornelis Bavelaar's carved-wood tableaux in the Hall

The Gallery

This corridor runs along the south side of the inner courtyard. It was built in the mid-18th century to connect the main ground-floor rooms.

Through the windows on the right, you can see the walls of the inner courtyard, which was rebuilt in the 1660s in red brick, in contrast to the earlier stone outer walls of the castle.

Pictures

To the right of the Hall door hangs a *watercolour copy of Van Dyck's famous equestrian portrait of Charles I*, painted by Bernard Lens in 1720. The Crofts were resolute supporters of the King during the Civil War.

The *family portraits* are mainly of 18th- and 19th-century Crofts, and are arranged in roughly chronological order clockwise from the Hall door.

Sir Herbert Croft, 1st Bt (*c.*1652–1720), married in 1675 *Elizabeth Archer* (d. 1709), who bore him eleven children, including their heir, *Sir Archer Croft, 2nd Bt* (1683–1753), who hangs here near his wife, *Frances Waring*. Sir Archer sold Croft Castle in 1746.

Sir Archer Croft, 3rd Bt (1731–92) settled at Dunston Park in Berkshire (his mother's family home) after Croft Castle was given up. He appears here in two portraits – painted in oil by Francis Cotes, and in pastel by Lewis Vaslet in Bath in 1781.

The Rev. Sir Herbert Croft, 5th Bt (1751–1816), never lived at Croft. He was nicknamed 'the Dictionary-maker', as he spent many years revising the famous dictionary compiled by his friend, Samuel Johnson, a bust of whom appears in the portrait by Lemuel Francis Abbott at the far end of the Gallery. However, Croft's revised version was never published, as he could not find enough subscribers to finance it. Abbott may also have painted the whimsical image of three of the Dictionary-maker's children as cherubim.

Sir Herbert Croft, 9th Bt (1838–1902), returned the family to Herefordshire after a long absence, settling at Lugwardine Court and serving as a local MP. The oil of him was painted about 1850 by Karl Hartman May, the chalk drawing by George Richmond in 1857.

Furniture

The six 1760s *chairs* are fine examples of the Gothick style, which applied the language of medieval church architecture – crockets, finials and quatrefoils – to the pierced backs and sides of domestic furniture.

John Kyrle (1637–1724), painted by Joseph van Aken, was nicknamed 'the Man of Ross', after the Herefordshire town where he lived frugally, giving much of his wealth to charity. The poet Alexander Pope praised Kyrle's philanthropy in his *Epistle to Bathurst*:

The Man of Ross divides the weekly bread:
He feeds yon almshouse, neat, but void of state.
...Is any sick? The Man of Ross relieves,
Prescribes, attends, the medicine makes, and gives.

Kyrle gave his name to the Kyrle Society, which was founded in 1875 to encourage the planting of trees and shrubs in cities, and was an important forerunner of the National Trust.

(Right) The Gallery

The Oak Room

This is the first in a sequence of rooms along the south front, which enjoys the best light and views. The room originally admitted even more light. But when the panelling and the sash-windows were installed in the early 18th century, the window to the left of the fireplace was covered up, although the light from it is still visible through a crack in the panelling.

In the mid-18th century, the suite of rooms was remodelled in the Gothick-Rococo style by Thomas Farnolls Pritchard. This became the 'dining parlour', which it remained until 1913. Pritchard painted the late 17th-century *panelling* white, but his paint was stripped off in 1913, when the fashion for bare wood was at its height.

Pritchard also designed the *ceiling plasterwork* with its trailing vine in the centre (an appropriate motif for a dining room) and four roundels at the corners filled with musical instruments and trophies. They were originally complemented by a Rococo *chimneypiece*, but this was moved to the Blue Room next door in 1913, when the present plain stone one was set up here. It was designed by Sarel in a convincing 17th-century style.

T. F. Pritchard's plasterwork ceiling roundel of musical instruments in the Oak Room

Dining at Croft in the 1760s

'The pleasures of the table played a highly important part at Croft Castle, and the tasty fare that arrived from [Captain Johnes at] Dolecothy was always joyfully welcomed. On one occasion we catch a glimpse of that formidable lady, Mrs Johnes, being so much carried away by the excellence of the Dolecothy fish and ducklings that at the end of the meal, when they had already eaten and drunk their fill, she insisted on calling for more wine and toasting each member of the Captain's family in bumpers.'

Elisabeth Inglis-Jones,
Peacocks in Paradise

Pictures

The *overmantel painting* depicts a Welsh landscape, possibly by George Barret (1728–84). He specialised in views of North Wales and of noble-men's estates painted in contrasting greens and yellows; his rival, the landscapist Richard Wilson, ridiculed the style as 'spinach and eggs'.

On the desk is a *silver-framed photograph* of Michael, 2nd Lord Croft and his sister Diana, taken in 1935.

The two *carved wood plaques* on the wall facing the fireplace depict the lion and wyvern (Welsh dragon) that form the two Croft family crests. Their Norman French mottoes below can be translated, 'To be

The Oak Room

rather than to seem to be' and 'Triumph over
death'.

On the wall to the right of the fireplace is a
vivid portrait of the 2nd Lord Croft painted in
1938–9 by Oskar Kokoschka. Lord Croft
introduced Kokoschka's art to Britain.

Furniture

The gilded and embossed *folding screen* from
Sherborne House, Gloucestershire, is covered in
'Spanish' leather.

Ceramics

The *porcelain figures* on the mantelpiece are
largely 18th-century Derby.

The Blue Room

The *Jacobean panelling*, according to family legend, was brought here in the 1760s by Thomas Johnes I from Stanage Park in Radnorshire. That house had been given to Johnes's wife, Elizabeth Knight, by her father on their marriage in 1746.

In the 1760s Pritchard painted the panelling blue, and most of his original paint survives. He also added the gilt rosettes and the painted shadows behind them, which were intended to enhance the three-dimensional effect. The original gilding was revealed beneath later layers of gold paint in 1984.

Pritchard was probably also responsible for the *ceiling plasterwork* with its scrolling Rococo decoration and Gothick detail at the centre. The *cornice* is adapted from illustrations in Batty Langley's *Gothic Architecture* (1747), an influential pattern book of the period, which was much derided by the aesthete Horace Walpole for trying to define individual Gothic orders of architecture on the classical model.

The *chimneypiece and overmantel*, which feature musical instruments and finely carved dog's heads, are the most ornate in the castle. They were carved in limewood about 1765 to Pritchard's design in the Shrewsbury workshop of Nelson and Van der Hagen. Sarel moved them here from the Oak Room in 1913. Pritchard's original, heavier chimneypiece may have been considered too funereal.

> 'The house is a very handsome one, a larger I never saw and there is here an elegant suit[e] of rooms, five in the same [style], it is surprising to see a suit[e] of rooms in an old country house.'
>
> Jane Johnes, a cousin who visited Croft in 1777

Pictures

Over the chimneypiece hangs *Elizabeth Cowper, Lady Croft* (1737?–1805), painted by Thomas Gainsbrough in Bath in 1761, when she was about 24. She had married Sir Archer Croft, 3rd Bt, in 1759, the year her portrait was also painted by Gainsborough's greatest rival, Sir Joshua Reynolds. She was a cousin of the poet William Cowper. Her daughter and son-in-law founded a new dynasty of Crofts at Greenham Lodge in Berkshire, with whom this portrait descended.

Furniture

One of the mid-18th-century high-back chairs is upholstered with a rare early 18th-century *embroidery of Delft flower-holders*, which were popularised in England by Queen Mary in the late 17th century. On the back of the chair is a pyramid vase similar to those still to be seen at Mary's principal palace, Hampton Court, and also at Dyrham Park in Gloucestershire. The much smaller fan-shaped vase on the seat resembles one at Uppark in West Sussex.

The *stumpwork box* of about 1640 is decorated with courtly scenes and is thought to be connected with Margery Croft, who served as maid of honour to Elizabeth, the 'Winter Queen' of Bohemia, or with Lucy Croft, who married Sir Dudley Carleton, the nephew of Charles I's ambassador in the Low Countries.

Ceramics

The *Worcester blue-and-white porcelain* was made in 1751–76, the era of Dr John Wall, who founded the Worcester factory.

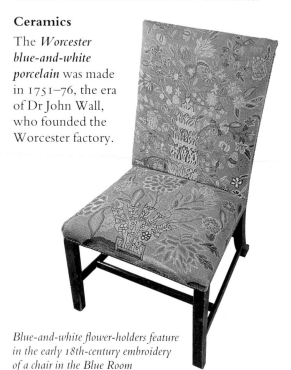

Blue-and-white flower-holders feature in the early 18th-century embroidery of a chair in the Blue Room

The Blue Room

The Saloon

The largest room in the castle is deliberately kept sparsely furnished so that it can be used for concerts and other events.

The *panelling* is early Georgian, like that in the Oak Room. Pritchard designed the *doorcases* in the 1760s, but two of them were moved here only in 1913, from 'Mr Johnes's dressing room'. (Thomas Johnes I gave up that ground-floor room to his formidable mother-in-law, Elizabeth Knight, when she was stricken with gout and could no longer climb the stairs.)

Pritchard also conceived the *plasterwork ceiling*, which features octagonal coffering inspired by the illustrations of classical ceilings in Robert Wood's *Ruins of Palmyra and Baalbec* (1753, 1757).

The *fireplace* was installed in 1913.

The National Trust repainted the room in 1987 to make it more in sympathy with the Blue Room next door. The late Lord Croft paid for the regilding.

Pictures

The *late 17th-century pastels* in baroque carved frames are said to depict Sir Herbert Croft, 1st Bt (c.1652–1720) and some of his eleven children, but only his father, the Bishop of Hereford, is definitely identifiable.

Furniture

The mahogany *square piano* was made in 1784 by William Southwell, who pioneered the upright form of the instrument. The Broadwood *grand piano* is late Georgian. The *set of Regency chairs*, c.1805, is in the Greek Revival style. They are placed back against the walls, as they would have been originally, when not in use. The chairs are part of the original furnishings of Finborough Hall, one of the grandest of Suffolk houses.

The *Dutch 'oyster' veneer cabinet* is early 18th-century.

The Library

The eight painted wooden bookcases, lettered from A to H, were designed for the room in the 1760s and have a frieze of Gothick quatrefoils. The walls were once painted jade green.

Books

The library, which is owned by the Croft Trust, comprises a comprehensive collection of books by and about the Crofts. A considerable number belonged to Sir Herbert Croft, 5th Bt, the 'Dictionary-maker'. They include his editions of Camden's *Britannia* and of Dr Johnson's famous dictionary, marked up with the

(Right) Thomas Johnes II published The Memoirs of John Lord de Joinville *(1807) at his private press at Hafod, which is illustrated on the title-page. The Library contains many of the Hafod Press's finest works*

MEMOIRS
OF
JOHN LORD DE JOINVILLE,
GRAND SENESCHAL OF CHAMPAGNE,
WRITTEN BY HIMSELF,
CONTAINING
A HISTORY OF PART OF THE LIFE OF LOUIS IX.
KING OF FRANCE, SURNAMED SAINT LOUIS,
INCLUDING AN ACCOUNT OF THAT KING'S EXPEDITION TO EGYPT IN THE YEAR MCCXLVIII,

To which are added,—the
NOTES & DISSERTATIONS OF M. DU CANGE ON THE ABOVE; TOGETHER WITH
THE DISSERTATIONS OF M. LE BARON DE LA BASTIE ON THE LIFE OF ST LOUIS,
M. L'EVESQUE DE LA RAVALIERE AND M. FALCONET
ON THE ASSASSINS OF SYRIA;
From the ' Memoires de l'Académie de Belles Lettres et Inscriptions de France.'

THE WHOLE TRANSLATED
BY THOMAS JOHNES, ESQ.

VOL. I.

At the hafod press.
BY JAMES HENDERSON.

MDCCCVII.

additions and corrections he planned to make in his revised version. The annotated dictionary is displayed here beside early compositions by Dr William Croft (1678–1727), who was organist at the Chapel Royal and a distant cousin of the Crofts of Croft Castle.

There is a group of rare early books on childbirth, such as *An Introduction to the Practice of Midwifery* (1801) by Thomas Denman, the most fashionable London gynaecologist of the period and the father-in-law of Sir Richard Croft, 6th Bt.

The library reflects the interests of Thomas Johnes II of Hafod, being particularly strong in works on local topography, architecture and landscape gardening, including the influential works on the Picturesque by his friend Uvedale Price and cousin Richard Payne Knight. There is a superb run of the publications of the Hafod Press, the private press founded by Johnes at his 'paradise' in west Wales.

Pictures

The portrait of the *2nd Lord Croft* (1916–97) was painted in the Library Ante-room by John Napper. It was commissioned by the National Trust in 1987. Photographs record the Second World War Council, of which the 1st Lord Croft was a member: and the 2nd Lord Croft with his children Charlotte and Bernard in the Library.

Sculpture

The bronze head on the window-sill is of *Diana Uhlman*, the sister of the 2nd Lord Croft. She lived at Croft for many years, enriched the Library and the collections, and wrote the previous edition of this guidebook.

Furniture

The *writing-table-cum-filing cabinet* left of the fireplace was known as 'The Croft' after Sir Herbert Croft, 5th Bt, for whom it was designed about 1780 by George Seddon. One cabinet was made for each letter of the alphabet.

Archaeological finds

In the corner turret are displayed some of the discoveries made during the excavation of the Iron Age hill-fort at Croft Ambrey (see p. 26).

A royal tragedy

Many of the images displayed here record the short life and tragic death of George IV's only child, *Princess Charlotte*. They include, in the right-hand window recess, a glass painting of her marriage in 1816 to Prince Leopold of Saxe-Coburg-Saarfeld (the future King of the Belgians). The young couple settled at Claremont in Surrey, and Charlotte was soon pregnant. On 5 November 1817 after an agonising labour, she delivered a still-born son (who would have been King of England, had he lived) and herself died the following day. Sir Richard Croft, 6th Bt, who was her attending physician, blamed himself for her death to such an extent that some months later he committed suicide. Sir Thomas Lawrence sketched his friend lying in his coffin, but with such discretion that he looks merely as though he is asleep. A copy of the drawing hangs over a door.

The Library Ante-room

This was conceived by T. F. Pritchard as part of the Gallery in the 1760s, when the three arched windows in the bay would have formed the focus to the east end of the Gallery. A generation later are the four slender mirrors that flank the windows, with their Gothick cluster columns and little fretted canopies. The walls would have been painted to match the mirrors, with a red band picked out above the black skirting.

The fireplace fills what was originally an open archway leading to the Gallery. The present pale green wall colour follows research into the late 18th-century decorative scheme.

Fireplace

The *Gothick overmantel* is another Pritchard design, which was brought here from the original library in the north wing. The fire surround is Derbyshire crinoid (fossil) marble.

The rare *transfer-printed tiles* in the fireplace were made by Sadler & Green in Liverpool in the 1760s. Some of the scenes on them were taken from illustrations in *The Ladies' Amusement* of c.1760, a popular source for such images.

Pictures

The great Regency portrait painter *Sir Thomas Lawrence* was a friend of Elizabeth Croft, who wrote an early memoir of him and inspired the good small collection of his work at Croft.

T. F. Pritchard's design for the Gothick overmantel mirror in the Library Ante-room

Isabella Wolff; by Sir Thomas Lawrence

About 1803 Lawrence painted the oval portrait of *Isabella Wolff*, who was the wife of the Danish vice-consul in London and also a close friend of the artist. The 1829 chalk drawing is of her son Hermann. In the display case is a self-portrait miniature, painted by Lawrence on ivory and set in a bracelet made of his hair.

Ceramics

The *pearlware busts* are of Princess Charlotte and her husband, Prince Leopold. The rectangular *japanned tinware dish* was probably made in the Pontypool factory, which was owned by the Hanbury-Williams family. The diplomat and aesthete Sir Charles Hanbury-Williams was a close friend of Thomas Johnes I in his youth.

Return to the Hall and walk back along the Gallery to reach the Dining Room.

(Right) Sadler & Green tiles in the Library Ante-room fireplace

The Dining Room

This room, which occupies the centre of the west range, was originally the west hall. In 1913 Walter Sarel transformed it into a mid-18th-century-style dining room. He inserted the Venetian window and the screen of columns – a typical 18th-century feature, intended to separate the area where food would be served from the main body of the room. To add to the 18th-century flavour, Sarel put up two pieces of Pritchard's original carving which had come from the Library: vases of flowers (over the chimneypiece) and swags (over the sideboard).

Pictures

The portrait of *Sir Richard Croft, 6th Bt* (1762–1818) was painted about 1804 by John James Hall (see p. 17).

The half-length portraits of *Henry, 1st Lord Croft* (1881–1947) and *his wife Nancy* (1883–1949) were painted by the leading society portraitist Philip de Laszlo in 1929 and 1924 respectively. Lord Croft had a turbulent career, aptly summarised in the title of his memoirs, *My Life of Strife*. During the First World War he served as a brigadier in the trenches before resigning his commission in 1916 to return to politics as MP for Bournemouth. In 1917 he helped to found the independent National Party, which campaigned to preserve the British Empire and to further the war effort. During the Second World War he was Under-Secretary of State for War. A dry-point etching of *Nancy, Lady Croft as a younger woman* by the French artist Paul Helleu also hangs nearby.

Furniture

The *Cumberland dining-table* is 19th-century. The *dining-chairs* are in the style of Thomas Chippendale.

Silver

The *Croft cups* on the sideboard are copies of 17th-century originals made for the daughters of Sir Archer Croft, 3rd Bt. The reproductions were made for the 1st Lord Croft's mother.

Return to the Gothick Stairs.

The Dining Room

The large group portrait of *The Children of Sir Richard Croft, 6th Bt* (on the near wall) was painted around 1803, possibly by Sir Martin Archer Shee. The children are (from left to right) Archer (1801–65), Frances (1800–77), Thomas (1798–1835), and, at the back with a book, Herbert (1793-1803).

Thomas holds a delicate china cup and blows a soap bubble from a clay pipe – both symbols of the fragility of young life. The references seem to have been personal, as there is a family tradition that the portrait of Herbert, who sits apart dressed in black, was painted posthumously.

George IV; by Sir Thomas Lawrence

Picture

The portrait at the foot of the stairs of *George IV* (1762–1830) was painted by Sir Thomas Lawrence. The King is shown still wearing mourning black in 1822, two years after the death of his father, George III, although the two men never got on. George IV was to spend huge sums in the 1820s redecorating Windsor Castle in the Gothick style. He refused to blame Sir Richard Croft, 6th Bt, when his only child, Princess Charlotte, died in childbirth while in Sir Richard's care (see p. 36).

Sculpture

The *marble bust* in the central niche is of Lord Denham, brother-in-law of Sir Richard Croft, 6th Bt.

The Corridor

The first-floor gallery is hung with changing displays from the present Lord Croft's collection of contemporary art, chosen and arranged by Lady Croft. They include interiors of Croft by Hector McDonnell and bronze heads of the present Lord Croft and his sister Charlotte as children by Georg Ehrlich.

The Gothick Stairs

This is the best surviving example of Thomas Farnolls Pritchard's Gothick work at Croft. Pritchard designed the quatrefoil frieze at half-landing level, the Gothick wall arches above with their ornate finials, the waterleaf cornice and the central ceiling rose, from which spring more Gothick arches. He was also responsible for the staircase itself, with its delicately carved banisters and tread ends.

Pritchard's scheme was obscured in the 19th century, but the husband of the 2nd Lord Croft's cousin, Mr Compton, revealed much of the detail in the 1970s, when the walls and ceiling were repainted close to their original colour.

From the bay window facing the bottom of the stairs, you get a good view into the internal courtyard, and of the 18th-century *fire-engine*.

The Corridor

The Ambassador's Room

Pritchard created this grand upstairs drawing room, which would have been used for music-making and dancing. The chimneypiece is one of his best efforts. The room takes its name from an Austrian ambassador, who was invited to stay at Croft around 1900, but in the event never turned up. Today, it commemorates the Johnes family's occupation of the castle in the second half of the 18th century.

Decoration

Edward Croft-Murray, an expert on historic decoration and a cousin of the family who had a flat in the castle, chose the wallpaper (a copy of a flamboyant early 18th-century pattern) and painted the bookcases.

Pictures and sculpture

The plaster bust by Sir Francis Chantrey on the window-sill and the crayon portrait over the door are both of **Thomas Johnes II** (1748–1816). He was brought up at Croft, whose ancient history and beautiful setting may have inspired him to transform Hafod from a remote wilderness in west Wales into one of the most ambitious of all Picturesque landscapes. There are also portraits of his Welsh Lloyd Johnes cousins, who lived at Dolaucothi.

Clock

The **gilt steeple clock** was made in the 16th century in Augsburg in Bavaria, which was one of the great European centres of high-quality goldsmiths' work in this period.

The Ambassador's Room

(Right)
The Augsburg gilt steeple clock,
c.1580 (Ambassador's Room)

(Far right)
The Samuel Green organ in the
Ambassador's Room

Furniture

The massive *chamber organ* was built in 1786 by Samuel Green, the foremost English maker of the period, and came from a neighbouring house. The early 18th-century *pier-glasses* between the windows are lent from Davenport House in Shropshire. The Chippendale gilt *overmantel mirror* originally hung at Sherborne House in Gloucestershire. The Chippendale chairs with embroidered seats (found stuffed with straw) are from Dolaucothi.

The East Staircase

Pictures

At the top of the stairs is a Welsh landscape by the painter Fred Uhlman, who left Germany in 1933 after the rise of Hitler and settled in Britain, where he married Diana Croft. The Uhlmans gave their collection of west African sculpture to the Hatton Art Gallery in Newcastle.

The *fifteen views of Hafod* depict the house and the surrounding Picturesque estate created by Thomas Johnes II in the late 18th century (see p. 34). J. C. Stadler's aquatints were based on watercolours painted by John 'Warwick' Smith during a visit to Hafod in the summer of 1792, and they helped to make the place famous.

The *watercolours of Cwm Elan* in Radnorshire show the valley that was drowned to create the reservoir that provides drinking water to Birmingham and the West Midlands.

The Gothick Bay Room

It matches the Library Ante-room on the opposite side of the Hall, and has a similar bay window, which was also added to the east front by Pritchard in the 1760s.

Pictures

The *engravings* include views of Croft Castle in 1792 (by J. Ross) and in 1840 (by Radclyffe). Wathen's hand-coloured engraving shows the west front of Hereford Cathedral after the central spire and tower collapsed in 1786.

Carl Laubin's 1989 painting reconstructs how Croft Castle would have looked before 1913, when Walter Sarel obscured much of its Gothick detail.

The *maps of Herefordshire* show how the county developed between 1570 and 1800.

The *Letters Patent* on vellum record the grants of land to Sir William Croft by James I in 1623.

Retrace your steps to the Hall to leave the castle.

Croft Ambrey

On a 300-metre high ridge to the north of the present castle lie the remains of the most elaborate Iron Age hill-fort in the Welsh Marches. It was an obvious spot to choose – a grassy triangular plateau defended on the north side by a steep natural drop. The fort was enclosed on the other sides initially by a single earth bank and ditch, which was later extended with a huge double rampart that cut through the enclosure. Excavation has uncovered decorative bronzework and a piece of gold chain, which hint at the wealth of the Celtic grain-farmers who built this fortress around 500 BC and farmed the landscape below. A granary building stored the fruits of their harvests.

By the time of the Roman invasion in the 1st century AD, the fort had probably been abandoned, although legend has it that the site was used by supporters of the rebel Celtic leader Caractacus. Certainly, the surrounding fields remained in cultivation, and some folk memory of this ancient settlement seems to have lingered on, as several shrines appear to have been set up on the site, drawing local people to worship here throughout the Romano-British era.

The Saxons founded a new settlement here, which took its name from the hilltop enclosure of Croft Ambrey. During the Middle Ages the ridge became a warren for rabbits, which were an important source of food and so were looked after by a warrener; the remains of his house and yard have been discovered. As a result, the ridge has never been ploughed, and the evidence of

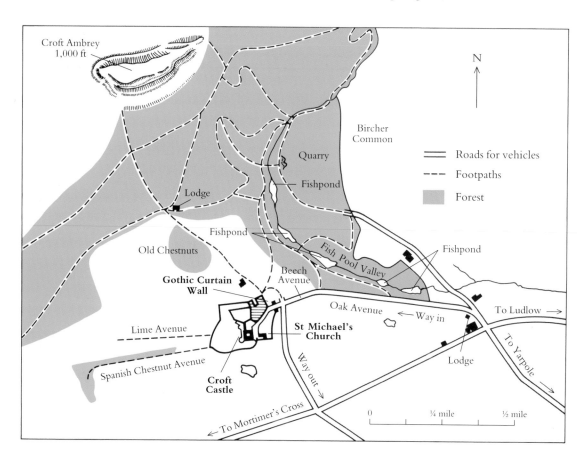

St Michael's church

this important early settlement has survived to be revealed by recent archaeology.

Today, Croft Ambrey is accessible from the castle via a path through the Forestry Commission plantations, and from its summit you can enjoy spectacular views west into Wales.

The Church of St Michael and All Angels

The church has always been part of one's first view of Croft; indeed, it predates the present castle, having been here, in some form, since at least the 12th century. For much of the medieval period, it was also the focus of a small village, which clustered on the slope to the south, but which has long since disappeared.

The present church probably dates from the 14th century. It was enlarged in the following century and remodelled in the 18th century. The pretty little bell turret was added in the late 17th century. In 1994 the church was reroofed in grey Welsh slate, replacing the inappropriate red tiles which had been put on in 1905.

The interior is lined with Jacobean panelling similar to that in the Hall of the castle. The boarded vault in the east bay was painted in the late 17th or early 18th century with clouds and gilded stars. The nave is filled with 18th-century box pews.

Monuments

The most elaborate of the Croft memorials is also the earliest – to Sir Richard (d. 1509) and Dame Eleanor Croft (d. 1520). Sir Richard is shown in armour with a tilting helm under his head and the heraldic Croft lion by his feet. The monument has clearly been moved around and reassembled during its long life, but the stone carving has survived in good condition and is of the highest quality – comparable, indeed, with the masons' work for the contemporary Henry VII Chapel in Westminster Abbey.

A more recent inhabitant of Croft is remembered in the stained glass of the east window: Herbert Kevill-Davies, who was killed fighting in the First World War. Two matching wall tablets side-by-side on the left-hand wall commemorate Crofts who also died in action: Sir Herbert Croft, 10th Bt, in the First World War, and his son, Sir James Croft, 11th Bt, in the Second World War.

The Grounds

The great glories of Croft are the sweeping views of the surrounding landscape and the ancient trees, some of which may date back to Elizabethan times. If so, they are relics of the first designed landscape here, which comprised oaks and chestnuts planted in groves and avenues, and a formal garden on the terrace to the south of the castle. When the castle was reconstructed in the late 17th century, the formal garden was extended to the west and south of the church.

In the mid-18th century formality was swept away and replaced, not with smooth parkland (the standard approach at the time), but with more rugged planting in the Picturesque style promoted by Richard Payne Knight and Uvedale Price, who were both friends of the Johnes family. In the last two centuries, little has been done to disturb this Picturesque vision, apart from the destruction in the early 19th century of a large Neo-classical orangery to the north-east of the castle.

The Oak Avenue

This runs roughly parallel to, and just to the north of, the entrance drive. The Croft oaks were already famous by 1808, when the *Leominster Guide* reported: 'Croft, Shobdon, Hampton and Brampton Brian Parks are famous for their large and majestic oak trees, which exceed in dimension those that grow in any other part of the kingdom.' Today, some have a girth of more than eight metres.

The Lime Avenue

The castle walls

The grey-brown limestone of the castle's walls is softened by roses, clematis and flowering shrubs such as *Itea ilicifolia*.

The Lime Avenues

Limes were planted on the entrance drive to the east of the castle around 1810. This is also the probable date of the entrance archway curtain wall and the refronting of the stables in the manner of John Nash, who was working in Herefordshire at the time. Very little of this avenue now survives, but, with the generous support of the Midland and Coventry National Trust centres, a new avenue has been planted to the west.

The Spanish Chestnut Avenue

The most venerable trees in this avenue were planted over 350 years ago, and are now gnarled and fissured with age. Running for about half a mile from the west front, they are arranged in a single and then triple lines, supposedly mimicking the battle formation of the Spanish Armada.

(Below) The view from the Fish Pool Valley towards Leominster in 1841; drawing by Edmund Gill

The Fish Pool Valley

This narrow valley was landscaped in the early 19th century in the Picturesque style. The stream was dammed to form a chain of artificial pools, and the valley sides were thickly planted with ash, oak, willow and poplar, together with evergreen species, to suggest the 'bold roughness of nature' championed by William Gilpin, Richard Payne Knight and other advocates of the Picturesque.

> To show the clear reflection of the day,
> And dart through hanging trees the refluent ray,
> And semi-lights and semi-shadows join
> And quiv'ring play in harmony divine.
>
> Richard Payne Knight, *The Landscape*, 1794

The Walled Garden

In 1979 Diana Uhlman, whose daughter manages this area of the garden, established a vineyard in the former kitchen garden. The family gives access to the garden, which rises high up the slope north of the castle, offering wonderful near and distant views, with the castle in the foreground.

Croft Castle and the Crofts

Early history

There have been Crofts at Croft since at least 1085, when the Domesday Book recorded one Bernard de Croft as the owner. By the end of the 14th century, the family had built themselves a fortified manor house a little to the west of the present house, as protection in this lawless border country. In the 1390s Sir John de Croft married one of the daughters of Owain Glyndŵr, who led the last serious Welsh revolt against English rule in 1400. Glyndŵr's rebellion was eventually crushed, which the Crofts' crest – a wounded black dragon – may have been intended to commemorate.

Sir Richard Croft (d. 1509)

Sir Richard is the first Croft of whom we have a portrait. The face that stares out from his tomb monument in Croft church is haggard – which is unsurprising, as he lived through the bloody era of the Wars of the Roses. Beside him lies his wife, Eleanor, who was the widow of a Mortimer from nearby Wigmore, one of the most powerful Marcher families of the period. In 1461 Sir Richard fought on the Yorkist side at the nearby battle of Mortimer's Cross, which established Edward IV (who was also a Mortimer) on the throne. Croft's loyalty to the Yorkist cause was rewarded with high office at the court which Edward IV set up in Ludlow. Eleanor served as governess to the King's two young sons, who are remembered in history as the 'Princes in the Tower'.

Sir Richard survived the overthrow of the Yorkists and the foundation in 1485 of the Tudor dynasty by Henry

VII, despite having been party to the execution of the new king's grandfather, Sir Owen Tudor. Indeed, like many Welsh landowners, he prospered, becoming Treasurer of the Royal Household and a Privy Counsellor. Croft was also appointed steward to the king's elder son, Prince Arthur, at Ludlow Castle, where the fifteen-year-old prince held court during the brief period between his marriage to Catherine of Aragon and his death from TB in 1502.

Sir James Croft (c.1518–90)

Sir Richard's great-grandson is the first member of the family of whom we have a painted portrait, which hangs in the Hall. Like Sir Richard and many of his descendants, James Croft was a soldier, fighting at the siege of

(Right) The tomb of Sir Richard and Eleanor Croft in St Michael's church

Sir James Croft, Controller of Elizabeth I's Household

Burghley, 'I assure you a man could not have got nearer a traitor and have missed, than Sir James'. Burghley himself considered that Croft's prickly temperament made him his own worst enemy. The Lord High Admiral, Charles Howard, was less charitable, dismissing him as 'a long grey beard with a white head witless'. Sir James represented Herefordshire in the Commons from 1563 until his death, when he was buried in Westminster Abbey. The antiquary William Camden gave him a diplomatic epitaph: 'He got above the envy of the court, which however had well nigh crushed him, and died in a good age, his Prince's favourite, and in fair esteem with all that knew him.'

It was probably Sir James who pulled down the medieval castle, which stood to the west of the present house, and rebuilt it as a small, but comfortable Elizabethan mansion more fitting his status. It was constructed from bricks made on site.

Edward Croft (d. 1601)

Sir James's son and heir followed him into Parliament as MP for Leominster and became embroiled in some of his political battles. When Sir James was arrested for alleged double-dealing in diplomatic negotiations with the Duke of Palma in 1588, Edward suspected the hand of Robert Dudley, Earl of Leicester, the Queen's former favourite, with whom Sir James had fallen out. In revenge, Edward is alleged to have employed a London conjuror, one John Smith, to cast a fatal spell on Leicester. When the Earl did actually die shortly afterwards, the younger Croft was charged with murder, but seems to have escaped conviction for one of the more bizarre Tudor plots.

As this episode suggests, Edward Croft was a reckless character, who was imprisoned for debt after his father's death. On his release, he fled to the Netherlands, where he spent the rest of his life. Perhaps because of his instability, he was never allowed to inherit Croft, which was put in trust for his son, Herbert.

Boulogne in 1544, where two of his brothers were killed. In 1547 he was knighted by Edward VI, who appointed him lord deputy of Ireland, which he tried unsuccessfully to pacify.

Sir James's fortunes changed for the worse with the accession of Queen Mary in 1553. He was implicated in Sir Thomas Wyatt's attempt to overthrow Mary and sent to the Tower of London, where the young Princess Elizabeth was a fellow prisoner. Despite being subjected to brutal cross-examination, he refused to implicate Elizabeth in the Wyatt plot. The princess never forgot Croft's loyalty at what was perhaps the most perilous moment of her career ('I stood in danger of my life,' she later admitted). When she became queen, she rewarded him with estates in Herefordshire and Kent and in 1570 made him Controller of the Royal Household. She also remained defiantly supportive when he fell out with many of her senior courtiers. In 1560 he was sacked as governor of Berwick, because he seemed to be getting too close to the warring Scots across the border. The Duke of Norfolk reported to Lord

Sir Herbert Croft (1566–1629)

Herbert Croft managed partially to restore the
family fortunes depleted by his father – by the
simplest expedient of marrying well. He tried to
win Barbara Gamage, a hugely wealthy heiress
from Glamorganshire, but was outbid by Robert
Sidney of Penshurst. He had to settle instead for
Mary Bourne, who eventually inherited the
Holt Castle estate in Worcestershire. Croft also
inherited the family weakness for argument,
pursuing a long-running feud with Thomas
Coningsby of nearby Hampton Court. Like
many of his family, he represented the local area
in Parliament, under both Elizabeth and James I,
who knighted him in 1603.

Croft was responsible for building the shell of
the present castle in the early 17th century. The
castle's turreted style is an early example of the
romantic 'medieval revival', which reflected the
Elizabethan and Jacobean fascination with a
chivalric past. He must have started work by
1616, because in that year he became a Catholic
and retired to the Benedictine monastery of
Douai in France. Here, according to one
witness, he was given 'a little cell within the
ambits of their house [and] spent the remainder
of his days therein in strict devotion and
religious exercise'. Despite his conversion, he
continued to profess his loyalty to King James.

Sir Herbert left behind three sons, all of
whom were to inherit Croft and all of whom
had to endure the turmoil of the Civil War.

Sir William Croft (1593–1645)

The Civil War

The eldest son, William, served as MP for
Malmesbury in 1623 and 1625. When the
argument between King and Parliament moved
from Westminster to the battlefield, he fought
on the Royalist side at the battle of Edgehill.
He had the respect of the King, who described
him as a man 'inured to great observations and
constant business from his childhood'. He was
captured by Parliamentary forces at Hereford in
1642 and held prisoner in Bristol until the
following year, when the city was taken by a
Royalist army.

*Charles I on horseback; an 18th-century watercolour copy of
Van Dyck's original painting. The Crofts were stalwart
supporters of the Royalist cause during the Civil War*

In 1644 Croft Castle was ransacked by Irish
mercenaries who had been employed by the
Royalist army and were disgruntled at not
having been paid. The Royalists dismantled all
except the outer walls of the castle to prevent it
being garrisoned by the Parliamentarians.
Personal tragedy followed swiftly on this
disaster. In June 1645 Sir William was part of a
Royalist force that encountered the enemy at
Stokesay Castle. After an hour's fighting, 100 of
his comrades lay dead and more than 350 had
been captured. Sir William fled the battlefield
and headed for home, closely pursued by the
Parliamentarians. After a ten-mile chase, they
finally caught up with him as he was about to
scale the park wall of Croft, and shot him dead.

Sir William was succeeded by his brother,
James, who was a colonel in the Royalist army.
With the castle in ruins, at the end of the war he
decided to settle in London, where he died, a
childless bachelor, in 1659. He left the Croft
estate to his younger brother Herbert, who was
to prove the most distinguished member of his
generation.

Herbert Croft, Bishop of Hereford (1603–91)

Privately, Herbert Croft shared the Catholic faith of his father, in 1626 being admitted to the English College in Rome under an assumed name. As this subterfuge suggests, it was a risky time to be a Catholic, and so he was persuaded to conform publicly to the tenets of the Church of England. About 1640 he was appointed chaplain to Charles I and in 1644 as Dean of Hereford. During the Civil War the cathedral was overrun by the Parliamentarians, who began stripping the altars. When Croft denounced this vandalism from the pulpit, some of the soldiers levelled their muskets at him, and were on the point of firing when their commander intervened. Croft survived, but lost all his church posts and would have been destitute if he had not succeeded to the remnants of the Croft estate on the death of his brother in 1659. His fortunes improved further the following year with the restoration of Charles II, who nominated him for the bishopric of Hereford in

1661. He served the diocese for the next 30 years, 'venerated … for his learning, doctrine, conversation, and good hospitality', according to one contemporary. The diarist Samuel Pepys described him in 1667 as 'an old good man, that they say made an excellent sermon'. Despite his earlier leanings, many of these sermons were devoted to denouncing Catholics. The job came with a grand bishop's palace in Hereford, but he preferred to live mainly at his ancient family seat at Croft, which he rebuilt out of his bishop's salary of £800 a year.

Sir Herbert Croft, 1st Bt (*c.*1652–1720)

The bishop's only son was created a baronet in 1671 as a reward for his family's loyal service to the Stuart cause, and four years later married Elizabeth Archer, the sister of the Warwickshire gentleman-architect Thomas Archer. She bore him eleven children, six of whom survived her. By the 1690s he was in poor health, staying at Tunbridge Wells to take the waters. By 1700 he was too frail to travel, and had given up his seat in Parliament, where he represented the county and was often at odds with the Harleys of Brampton Bryan, but he lived on for another 20 years.

Sir Archer Croft, 2nd Bt (1683–1753)

In 1720 Sir Archer Croft was one of many speculators who got their fingers burnt when the South Sea Bubble burst. His finances never really recovered, despite his best efforts. He was MP for Leominster from 1722, and by grovelling letters managed to ingratiate himself with the Prime Minster Sir Robert Walpole, who rewarded him with a lucrative job on the Board of Trade. In 1739 he was appointed governor of New York, which was already a thriving port, but he never felt the need to cross the Atlantic. Despite retiring from politics in 1734 with a pension of £1,000, he got into such serious debt that he was forced to mortgage, and then in 1746 to sell, the Croft estate to Richard Knight of nearby Downton.

Herbert Croft, Bishop of Hereford

Richard Knight

New blood

Knight's wealth derived from the new industry of iron. His family managed ironworks at Coalbrookdale in Shropshire (the crucible of the Industrial Revolution) and later at Wolverley in Worcestershire. But in their architectural tastes, the Knights looked to the past and the Picturesque. One of his nephews was Edward Knight, who was an admirer of Sanderson Miller, the gentleman-architect of Gothick mansions and follies. Another was Richard Payne Knight, who was to rebuild Downton Castle as a mock-Gothic fortress in the 1770s.

Richard Knight bought Croft in 1746, not primarily for himself, but for his only child and heir, Elizabeth, and her husband, Thomas Johnes, whom she married the same year.

Thomas Johnes I (c.1721–80)

Making Croft more Gothic

In his youth Thomas Johnes was a leading figure in fashionable London society, being a close friend of the politician Richard Fox. On his marriage he moved to Herefordshire, where he entertained on a grand scale. He seems to

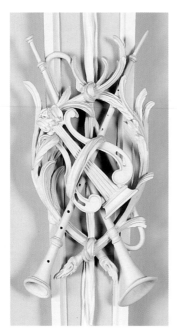

The superb carved-wood trophy of musical instruments on the Blue Room overmantel is part of T. F. Pritchard's 1760s Gothick redecoration of the castle

have lived somewhat in the shadow of his wife, Elizabeth, a strong-willed woman worth £70,000, who kept tight hold on the purse strings.

Little had been done to Jacobean Croft Castle for a century, and by the 1760s it must have been looking somewhat dowdy. Johnes decided to redecorate the castle in the Rococo-Gothick style, which he must have felt was appropriate to the castle's medieval origins. He may have been encouraged in his choice by his friend, John, 2nd Viscount Bateman of nearby Shobdon, where the parish church had been remodelled in a version of this style in 1752–6. Johnes chose as his architect a local man, Thomas Farnolls Pritchard of Shrewsbury. Today, Pritchard is chiefly remembered as the designer of the world's first iron bridge, at Coalbrookdale in Shropshire, but he also did much country-house work in the area. An album in Washington preserves Pritchard's elegant designs for Gothick doorcases and overmantels for Croft, which his craftsmen translated into carved wood with supreme skill. Later rearrangement has somewhat diminished and obscured Pritchard's achievement at Croft, but much still survives on the staircase and in the principal ground-floor suite along the south front. It is his work that gives the interiors at Croft their particular fascination.

Thomas Johnes II (1748–1816) of Hafod

Creating a paradise in Wales

The Johneses' eldest son Thomas was brought up at Croft, which can only have helped to fuel his fascination with the Middle Ages. He also had a dream of creating a Picturesque landscape in the remote wilderness of west Cardiganshire, urged on by the two most influential pundits of the Picturesque, his cousin Richard Payne Knight and his friend Uvedale Price. Price shared his love of the Gothic, commissioning a neo-Gothic summer villa in the grounds of the ruined Aberystwyth Castle. The heir to three separate fortunes, Thomas Johnes II had the means to translate his dream into reality. He chose a wild spot at Hafod in the Ystwyth

(Right) View of Hafod House; aquatint by J. C. Stadler after John 'Warwick' Smith, 1792. The house burnt down in 1807, but was rebuilt shortly afterwards by Thomas Johnes II

valley, where he planted over six million trees to create a model estate. Carefully arranged walks across valley and mountain exploited the sublime drama of the Devil's Bridge and the Falls of Mynach, which Turner and numerous other artists came to record. The watercolourist George Cumberland called it 'the sweetest interchange of hill and valley, rivers, woods and plains, and falls with forest, crown'd, rocks, dens, and caves'. The Hafod dairy produced Parmesan, Stilton, Gloucester and Cheshire cheeses 'so excellent in quality, and so exact in the imitation of shape and flavour, as to deceive the most accurate eye or palate.'

At the heart of the estate was the house designed by Thomas Baldwin of Bath and John Nash, which Johnes filled with beautiful things. The octagonal library contained a priceless collection of early Welsh manuscripts and the publications of his private press, which included his own translation of Froissart, the great chronicler of the Hundred Years War. On the terraces outside, peacocks shrieked and merino sheep cropped the lawns.

The Hafod dream gradually turned into a nightmare. Johnes's spending ran out of control to such an extent that he was obliged to sell the Croft estate in the 1780s, forcing his furious mother to retire to London. In 1807 Hafod House and its precious library burnt to the ground, and – worst of all – in 1811 his beloved only child Marianne died. Today, Hafod House has gone, and the park is surrounded by unromantic Forestry Commission plantations, but you can still glimpse in the views displayed on the East Staircase at Croft something of the place's special magic, which the Hafod Trust is working to restore.

And here were gardens bright with sinuous rills,
Where blossomed many an incense-bearing tree;
And here were forests ancient as the hills,
Enfolding sunny spots of greenery.

From Coleridge's *Kubla Khan*, which may have been partly inspired by Hafod

Thomas Johnes II, who was brought up at Croft and created a famous model estate at Hafod; bust by Sir Francis Chantrey

The Crofts in exile

The 2nd Baronet's son, another Archer (1731–92), moved from Croft to his mother's family home, Dunston Park in Berkshire. In 1759 he married Elizabeth Cowper, who was a cousin of the poet William Cowper and was painted by both Reynolds and Gainsborough. Their son died young, and so on Sir Archer's death in 1792, the title passed to his brother John, and shortly afterwards to a cousin.

Rev. Sir Herbert Croft, 5th Bt (1751–1816)

The Dictionary-maker

He trained as a lawyer, but could not afford to pursue a legal career, and so took holy orders. He settled in Oxford, where he devoted years to revising the famous dictionary compiled by his friend Samuel Johnson. But Sir Herbert was a volatile character, who found it difficult to finish projects, and his revision was never published. (Despite this, he was always known in the family as the 'Dictionary-maker'.) He was also a hopeless spendthrift: on the day after his second marriage in 1795, he was arrested for debt. He managed to flee the country and spent most of his remaining years in exile in France. He inherited the title in 1797, but it made little difference, as the estates had passed to others.

Sir Richard Croft, 6th Bt (1762–1818)

A royal catastrophe

Sir Herbert's younger brother and heir had a much more successful career, but it also ended in ignominy. He became one of the leading obstetricians in Regency London, having inherited the fashionable practice of his father-in-law Dr Thomas Denman. Sir Richard made his name after attending the Duchess of Devonshire at the birth of her son (later the Bachelor 6th Duke) in 1790.

Such was Sir Richard's reputation that he was chosen in 1817 to look after the Prince Regent's only child, Princess Charlotte, during her pregnancy. On 3 November the Princess went into labour when already 42 weeks pregnant. After a ghastly 50-hour labour, she finally delivered a 9lb baby boy, but he was still-born; if he had lived, he would in due course have become King of England, and there would have been no Victorian age. Charlotte seemed at first to have survived the ordeal, but she began to haemorrhage and at 2.30am the following day she also died. By the primitive standards of the day, Sir Richard had done all he could, and the Prince Regent did not blame him for the tragedy, but he became the victim of a media witchhunt from those who thought he should have attempted a forceps delivery. Sir Richard himself took all this criticism personally, and

(Far left) Elizabeth, Lady Croft; by Thomas Gainsborough

(Left) The Rev. Sir Herbert Croft, 5th Bt, the Dictionary-maker

Princess Charlotte ascends to heaven; pen and wash drawing attributed to E. F. Burney. The princess's death in childbirth in 1817 provoked an outpouring of public grief

when another of his patients died in childbirth the following year, he shot himself. The painter Thomas Lawrence drew a touching posthumous portrait of his friend lying in his coffin. A facsimile hangs in the Library.

Croft Castle in the Victorian and Edwardian eras

Thomas Johnes had sold the Croft Castle estate to Somerset Davies, who was a prosperous Ludlow mercer and alderman, and also MP for the town. The Davies family already owned the best house in Ludlow (which had been remodelled by Pritchard) and Wigmore Hall in Shropshire, and so for part of the next century, the castle was rented out. Despite this, the family still felt strong enough ties with Croft to commemorate their dead in Croft church. The east window remembers Herbert Kevill-Davies, who was killed in the First World War.

The castle transformed

In 1913 the tenant, Major Atherley, commissioned the architect Walter Sarel to modernise the castle. Much of his work was practical,

The Edwardian architect Walter Sarel remodelled the castle in 1913. The work was done by W. H. Gaze & Sons

This is a photograph of the historic CROFT CASTLE, reconstructed and decorated by W. H. GAZE & SONS, LTD.

and heir, another Herbert, was commissioned into the Herefordshire Regiment at the relatively advanced age of 46 on the outbreak of the First World War in 1914. A year later, he was killed leading his company during the bloody landings that opened the disastrous Gallipoli campaign.

The second Sir Herbert's infant son James succeeded to the title in 1915, and he was still a child in 1923, when his trustees decided to buy back the Croft Castle estate after a gap of over 170 years. To make the castle more practical, they decided to demolish the old service wing in 1937. But holding on to Croft during the following years of war and austerity was to prove a complex and difficult task.

Sir James Croft, 11th Bt, enjoyed his new home only briefly, as he also died in war. Having survived the Norway campaign, he was killed in Scotland in 1941 while training with No.1 Commando. The childless Sir James bequeathed Croft to his cousin, Sir Henry Page

Sir Henry Page Croft, 1st Lord Croft; by Philip de Laszlo

(Right) Michael, 2nd Lord Croft in front of the Library Ante-room fireplace; by John Napper

installing new services and adding a porch on the entrance front to keep out the draughts. He also tried to tone down the spikier excesses of Pritchard's Gothick decoration. But few now consider the Jacobethan panelling and bland stone fireplaces that he put up to have been an improvement, and in recent years the Trust has attempted to restore some elements of Pritchard's work.

The Crofts return to Croft

The 6th Baronet's grandson, Sir Herbert Croft, 9th Bt (1838–1902), began the Croft family's gradual return to their ancestral home by settling at Lugwardine Court near Hereford and serving as MP for the area. His son

Croft, 1st Lord Croft, because he reckoned that Lord Croft would be the member of the family best able to keep the estate going. Sir James, however, failed to warn his cousin of the bequest, which came as a considerable shock. At the time he inherited, Lord Croft was Under-Secretary of State for War in Churchill's wartime government, and coming to the end of a long and turbulent political career.

During the First World War, he had served with great distinction in the trenches, commanding a brigade in the Battle of the Somme. However, he was persuaded that he could better serve the war effort by returning to Parliament. In 1917 he helped to found the independent National Party, which sought to preserve the British Empire. Throughout the inter-war years, Sir Henry retained his Bournemouth seat as an Independent, and then a Tory, supporting Churchill's campaign against Indian self-government.

Croft was at its lowest ebb when Sir Henry inherited. During the Second World War the house was occupied by a convent school. He finally came properly into his inheritance aged 65 only in December 1946, when the staff laid on a welcome home party. He began the urgent task of mending the roof and reviving the shabby decoration, but he died the following year before he could complete it.

His son Michael, who became the 2nd Lord Croft, had bought back the remainder of the ancient estate in 1942, but his father's death once again put Croft in jeopardy, as the estate faced crippling death duties. Lord Croft thought that the only way to keep Croft in the family was to sell the estate to his cousin, Major Owen Croft, the family's historian. However, Major Croft was not a wealthy man, and on his death in 1956, his widow Stella felt obliged to sell up. The estate was once more under threat.

Croft was saved only by the combined efforts of several different parties: the National Land Fund, which had been set up to honour the memory of the war dead (who included two members of the Croft family); the National Trust; and, equally important, the Croft family. Lord Croft's sister, Diana Uhlman, led the campaign, rallying the support of Christopher Hussey, the influential architectural editor of *Country Life*. Lord Croft endowed the castle, supported by Mrs Uhlman and a public appeal, and provided furniture, carpets, curtains, chandeliers and many important family portraits. He also encouraged his sister Diana to set up the Croft Trust to rescue furniture, books and other items connected with the castle for display here. The most important of these is probably Gainsborough's portrait of Lady Croft in the Blue Room (illustrated on p. 36), acquired by Lord Croft with the help of his relations. Lord Croft was himself a discerning collector of British art, being appointed an honorary keeper of the Fitzwilliam Museum in Cambridge, to which he left eight beautiful watercolours by Paul Nash on his death in 1997.

The present Lord Croft, with his wife, and a cousin, Mrs Compton, still lives at Croft, maintaining the family presence that stretches back a millennium to his namesake, Bernard de Croft.

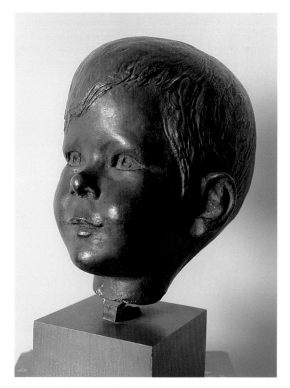

Bernard, 3rd Lord Croft as a boy

The Crofts of Croft Castle

BERNARD DE CROFT
Held Croft in 1086
⋮

Sir RICHARD CROFT† = Eleanor Mortimer†
(1487–1509) │ née Cornewall (d. 1520)

Sir EDWARD CROFT = Joyce Skull
(d. 1547)

RICHARD CROFT = Katherine Herbert
(d. 1562)

Sir JAMES CROFT* MP = (1) Alice Wigmore, née Warnecombe
(c.1518–90) │ (d. 1573) m. c.1540
(2) Catherine Blount

EDWARD CROFT, MP = Anne Browne
(d. 1601) │ (d. 1575)

Sir HERBERT CROFT, MP = Mary Bourne
(1566–1629)

| Sir WILLIAM CROFT, MP (1593–1645) | Sir JAMES CROFT (d. 1659) | Dr HERBERT CROFT* Bishop of Hereford (1603–91) = Anne Browne | Elizabeth Croft* (d. 1622) | (2) Lucy Croft (c.1608–48) grandmother of architect Sir John Vanbrugh = Sir Dudley Carleton |

Sir HERBERT CROFT, MP* = Elizabeth Archer (d. 1709) m. 1675
cr. 1st Bt 1671 (c.1652–1720) │ sister of architect Thomas Archer

| Sir ARCHER CROFT 2nd Bt, MP* (1683–1753) *Sells Croft 1746* = Frances Waring* (d. 1767) m. 1723 | 3 daus. | Francis Croft (d. 1724) = Grace Bramston | 6 sons |

| Sir Archer Croft, 3rd Bt* (1731–92) = Elizabeth Cowper* (1737?–1805) m. 1759 | Sir John Croft, 4th Bt (c.1735–97) | Herbert Croft (d. 1785) = (1) Elizabeth Young (2) Mary Chawner |

| Rev. Sir Herbert Croft, 5th Bt* (1751–1816) 'Dictionary-maker' = (1) Sophia Clere (d. 1792) (2) Elizabeth Lewis (d. 1815) m. 1795 | Sir Richard Croft, 6th Bt* (1762–1818) *Royal physician* = Margaret Denman (d. 1847) | Elizabeth Croft (1769–1859) |

| Sir Thomas Croft, 7th Bt* (1798–1835) = Sophia Lateward (d. 1890) m. 1824 | Sir Archer Croft, 8th Bt* (1801–65) m. 1837 = Julia Corbet (d. 1864) | Rev. Richard Croft (d. 1869) = (1) Charlotte Russell |

| Grace (d. 1898) = Edward Murray | Sir Herbert Croft, 9th Bt, MP* (1838–1902) m. 1865 = Georgina Marsh | Richard Croft (d.1912) of Fanhams Hall = Anne Page |

| Bernard Croft-Murray = Amy James | Sir Herbert Croft, 10th Bt* (1868–1915) = (1) Kathleen Hare (d. 1898) m. 1892 (2) Katherine Parr m. 1903 | Sir Hugh Croft, 12th Bt (d. 1954) = Lucy Taylor | Major OWEN CROFT* (1880–1956) = Stella Bouwer | Brig.-Gen. Sir HENRY PAGE CROFT, MP* 1st LORD CROFT (1881–1947) = Hon. Nancy Borwick (1883–1949) | Lt. Col. Richard Page Croft (d. 1956) = Eva Waithman |

| Edward Croft-Murray | Sir JAMES CROFT, 11th Bt* (d. 1941) *His trustees buy back Croft 1923* | Sir Bernard Croft, 13th Bt = Helen Weaver | MICHAEL, 2nd LORD CROFT* (1916–97) = Lady Antoinette Conyngham (d. 1959) m. 1948 | Hon. Diana Croft = Fred Uhlman | Major Richard Page Croft = Peggy McClymont |

Bernard, 3rd Lord Croft* = Mary Richardson
(b. 1949)   m. 1993

Caroline   Hugo

Owners of Croft are in CAPITALS
* denotes portrait on show
† denotes memorial in the church

40